where the water flows

arlyne soto

where the water flows

Copyright © 2024 arlyne soto
All rights reserved.

deeper ◎ truths

ISBN: 979-8-3303-0247-5

Layout Design by: Rein G.
@reindrawthings (www.fiverr.com)

dedication

to anyone who has ever loved.

TABLE OF CONTENTS

What do you fear?

I fear being wrong.

I fear not being enough.

I fear being draining.

I fear pulling you away from happiness.

I fear pulling you down with me.

I fear being fully vulnerable.
Which is why I'm constantly on edge,
waiting for the next thing to destroy me.

I fear being assertive,
and being refused of my needs and wants.

I fear of not being worthy of the love
I am receiving.

I fear not being fully loved.

But then,

I look at you.

I feel your being.
Your light,
your life.

And that fear
when I let it
lifts away.

When you tell me
"breathe"
"Let go"
"I love you"
I can feel the universe.

When you hold me tight,
gently grab my hand,
kiss me softly on the lips,
kiss me softly on my forehead.
The words are reinforced.

I didn't think I could love someone
so much.

So much that my fear of
destroying the beautiful being
in front of me,
creates a toxic water that I drink.

Toxic water I don't realize I'm drinking.

Toxic water of the past,
of negative energies,
of self-doubts,
of feelings that I am not worthy.

But I am.

I am worthy of all this light,
all this beauty.

What can I do to show myself that?

That's the real question.

Dear lover,

I'm writing this before I hear about what you decided for us. After I left last night, I was in so much pain. I didn't know what to do or what to expect. I think back and wonder what more I could have done to understand. Now, when I think back, I think about how the thoughts you were having were anxious thoughts. It makes some sense as to why they had become more intense and triggering. I was talking about a potential trip for the both of us that can either be enjoyable or show the lapses in our relationship. I think now that maybe you just needed some reassurance, that your worried thoughts are normal. I think now you needed me to stay and fight, not to give into your thoughts, which you had done for me so many times. I'm sorry I wasn't there for you. I wonder if that could have changed anything, but I wanted to respect your request for space. The struggle to not reach out to you and have us talk it through, or have one last hug, or cuddle or kiss, is fucking excruciating. I'm trying not to think of the end but it's hard not to. I too failed to be more supportive. All I want right now is for you to be physically near me. I'm sorry for not being more aware and present of you pulling away. I have no idea what is going to happen to us. All I know is that right now, I can't seem to stop from crying and my heart definitely feels as though it's breaking.

I can't help but think, for the safety of my broken heart, that we'll push through. That you'll be ready to try and continue. God, this is so painful. Painful because maybe what you said has some truth. Maybe we aren't going to make it? Maybe we are different? But maybe we aren't so different that even that is terrifying. I love you lover, so much. Thank you for loving me, for trying to love me. Thank you for showing me I can fall in love again. Whatever you choose, I will support it. However, it doesn't mean I won't need my own space to heal and recover as well. Again, thank you lover for all that we had and if you so choose, potentially more.

I hope you find what you're looking for otherwise.

Maybe I'll just write to you in my journal.

I'll write about how wild that episode of *The Outsider*
was and how I wish we watched it together.

I'll write about how I listened to some new music
today that I thought you'd like.

I'll write about how I checked my phone to see
if you texted me.

I'll write about how everyone keeps commenting
on the boots you bought me and how cute they are.

I'll write about how the kids were wonderful today.

I'll write about how I tried to help calm a crying
preschooler by having her feel my breathing
and could only think of you doing that for me.
How I was starting to get teary thinking back
to the memory.

I'll write about how much I really just wanted to
go on a run today.

I'll write about how when the teachers asked me
how I am,
I got choked up and started to cry.

I'll write about how listening to the sleep music at
nap time brings me back to New Years in your room.

I'll write about how much I miss you and just want
to hear you voice.

I'll write about how I want you to say you miss me too.

I'll write about how hard it is to keep back the tears.

I'll write about how much I still think about you.

I'll write about how you're the first thing on my mind
in the morning.

I'll write about how hurt and sad I'm feeling right now.

I'll write about how I wonder how you're doing.

I'll write about how I wonder if you're hurting
just like me.

I'll write about how I wonder if you want me
to come over.

I'll write about how I wonder if you miss my touch
as much as I miss yours.

I'll write about how I wonder if we could ever
be friends.

I'll write about how I wonder if I could be able
to somehow keep you in my life without wanting
you too.

I'll write about how I am literally aching.
How I'm hurting for you again.

I'll write about how it still hurts me
to reminisce about you physically pulling away.

I'll write about how much I still love you.
How much I still want you.

I'll write about how shitty this is.

I'll write about how I can see the healthy and maybe
not so healthy parts of our relationship and still want
to try.

I'll write about even if you'd ask to try again right now.
I'd say no.

I'll write about how I hope you're doing well.

I'll write about how I hope you're spending time
with friends and working on yourself.

I'll write about how I hope you hope the same for me.

I'll write about how I don't want to stop writing
to you but I know I have to.

I'll write about I don't know what the future holds
but I'm going to keep on focusing on me.

I'll write about I don't know how long I'd love you
for but right now it feels like forever.

I'll write about how I'm already thinking about
trying to reach out in a few months.

I'll write about how I don't think that's a good idea
and how you'd probably agree.

I'd write about how hard it is to not try
and reach out or look up on social media.

I'll write about how I wonder if this will get easier.

I'll write about how I wonder
when I'll stop writing to you.

I'll write about how I still love you.

I'll write about how I hope these letters to you
will stop soon.

I'll write about how I hope this gets easier.

I'll write about how I love you so much.

I'll write about how sometimes I still think
you are my person.

I'll write about how I sometimes don't want
to think about that.

I'll write about how I hope we are able
to talk again.
But not anytime soon.

I'll write about how I don't know what I'm going
to do in the future anymore.

I'll write about how I want to tell you and ask you
if I should move away.

I'll write about how if I do I want you to say
"no, stay."

I'll write about how I hope I get over you soon.

I'll write about,
how much I still love you.

How much I know I will.

How much time it'll take to heal.

How I can't promise I can be a friend.

How maybe I'll just be cheering for you
from a distance.

I'll write about how I'm going to put myself first.

I'll write about how sometimes it's hard
to accept you're not with me anymore.

I'll write about how I'll keep trying to move forward.

I'll write about how hopefully, the letters stop.

And I can finally breathe again.

How is this not killing you?

How is this not killing your very being?

I literally don't think I can cry out all the pain
I'm feeling right now.

I wonder what you're doing tonight.

I like to think you're at home,
making some art to describe the pain
and hurt you feel.

But then I think maybe you're numbing yourself,
you're out with friends,
pretending everything is fine,
and drinking the pain away.

Or maybe you are doing fine.

Part of me doesn't want to believe or envision that.

This is so weird.

Isn't it weird for you?

All I want right now is to be with you.

I just want to be sitting on your couch,
watching some random show.

Or out with your friends,
at the bar,
playing pool,
whatever activity they choose.

I want to talk to you so badly.

I want to tell you about my day and how
all I think about is you.

How right now I feel pathetic,
that I'm at home,
crying on my bed and wishing
you were still here.

Why is this so hard?

Why is heartbreak so painful?

I keep thinking about what you said,
about how maybe this is the wrong time.

Did you really mean that?

Or were you saying that to help ease the pain?

I know you really loved me Lover.

That couldn't be fake.

I know my love for you is real,
otherwise I wouldn't be writing out
my thoughts,
writing out my pain.

I'm really hoping this will get easier.

But right now,
knowing I'm not going to your place tonight,
knowing that you're not coming here,
makes the pain feel like it never left.

God,

I just keep wanting to say that I love you.

But that feels pathetic too.

I wonder how long it will be for you to come
to terms with the end of us?

Would it be quicker?
Would it be longer?

Right now, I just want to know if you feel
like how I'm feeling right now.

Holding back the screams,
holding back the shaking sobs.

And as much as I want you to be suffering with me,
I hope you're having fun Lover.
I hope your laughing with your friends
and smiling about this wonderful life we have.

I hope you're not thinking about how I'm doing
because I don't think you'll like what you see.

Because as much as I want the suffering
to be the same,
I love you so much that I want you to be happy.

I want you to be bright and beautiful.

I still think about how I called you
"my person."

I wonder if that will be true.

Because when I said it,
it was truly what I felt and believed.

I wonder if you will stay in my life.

I don't know what the future holds,
but right now,
I want you in it.

And maybe,
maybe after some months have past,
I won't even think about you anymore.

Maybe we'll never speak again.

Right now,
that aches my core.

But, maybe that will happen.

Maybe,
maybe we'll reconnect and become the best of friends.

Maybe we'll bump into each other at a festival,
a concert,
a bar,
a restaurant,
and our hearts will fall again.

Maybe,
maybe you'll have to fail a few more times
before you find your one.

Maybe you have to fail a few more times
to find your way back to me.

Maybe,
maybe I'll never see you again.

I think writing down all these possibilities helps a bit.

But,
all I know right now,

is I want you,

right here,

right now,

I want your smile,
your laugh,
your jokes,
your stunning stares,

I want to talk to you like nothing ever happened.

I want to tell you about everything that's happened
in these past days,
I want to let you know about every time I missed
and thought about you.

I wonder how long I'll love you for.

I wonder how long this feeling will last.

And I've noticed that the more times I write to you,
the harder it is to stop.

Because I know when it stops,
it makes it all that much more real,

that you're not here to share this with.

Do you think I'm pathetic?

I don't think I could hear you say that,
I don't think this is easier for you either.

But for some odd reason,
I keep thinking,
you're happy and living life,
you're not even thinking about us anymore.

Maybe it's because thinking you already moved on,
will help me move on too.

Because otherwise,
why are we torturing ourselves?

I didn't think I could fall
for someone so quickly.

You stole my heart.

Everything is still so painful to accept
that we're not us anymore.

My heart aches to hear your voice,
to hear you laugh,
to see your scrunched-up face in a grin,
to watch you dance all goofy,
to see you acrobat your way through your home,
to smell your musky sweet earthy smell,
to experience your pure concentration envelope
your face,
to feel your touch,
to accept your embrace,
to feel you lips on mine,
to purposefully and awkwardly kiss
with our tongues.

I miss all of you.
I miss your sassiness,
your odd and random thoughts about life,
your stubbornness,

your competitiveness,
your brilliant mind,
your devotion and strive toward the planet,
your incredible ability to create,
your humor and dad jokes,
your adoration,
your gentle and beautifully kind nature,
your fears and insecurities,
your ability to make me fall for you ever day.

Will this feeling ever go away?

I feel like the more I talk about it,
talk about you,
the more hope I instill,

that this isn't the end of our story.

But,

I should accept it.
I know I can't hold on to that hope,
that possibility.

I love you.

I miss you.

I miss you so much,

you'll always be my beautiful stranger.

I want you to reach out,

but I don't.

I want you to send me likes or watch my stories,
but I don't.

I want you to tell me that you want me and miss me.
But I don't.

I want you to see that your friends are still in touch,
and give you the urge to stay in touch too.

But I don't.

I want you to call me, FaceTime me so we can talk
about this crazy quarantine,
But I don't.

I still want you so badly,
but I don't.

I want you to be my friend and we can talk like before.
But I don't.
Because I can't.

I can't keep reaching out and hoping.

Because that's not fair.

To me or to you.

No matter how much I still want you here.

I keep writing about how I hope this gets easier.

I keep writing about how I just want you here.

I keep writing about how I still feel and think
you're my person.

I keep writing about how I hope you are happy
and in love with life.

I need to start writing that for myself.

I need to start focusing more on my health.

I need to start focusing on my future.

This life that's unfolding.

I am still so aching,
and hurting,
and yearning.

Are you?

Do you still think about me?

Do you still think about us?

Do you wish things would have been different?

Do you ever want me back?

No,

I hope you don't have those thoughts.

I hope you have rid of me.

I hope the love you have for me dies into a friendship.

Because still loving you,

is hurting me.

I wish this were easier.

This timing honestly couldn't have been any harder.

Especially with everything that's going on.

I do wonder if it's hard for you too.

I love you.

I hope that will get easier to stop saying each time
I write to you.

I wonder what you're doing to help this process
of heartbreak.

Sometimes, I think I should do what you do.
Numb and pretend it never happened.

But then I don't think I'll ever move past.
I really hope the best for you.

And as much as I want it,

I really hope you just leave me alone.

I Thought You Were My Person...

I keep thinking about the night where,
we were laying in my bed,
your head in my arms,
I apologized for being so distant,
and as I cried,
I told you "I think you're my person."

I thought you were the person
I was supposed to grow with.

I thought you were the person
I was supposed to explore,
the ends of the earth with.

I thought you were my everything.

I feel as heartbroken as I did the night
you pulled away.

The night you told me,
you weren't going to stay.

I thought you were going to be my everything.

I thought you were mine.

Mine to love and be free.

I wonder if you ever think about that night.

If you ever think about me.

If it ever rips you up inside,
and you cry for me too.

Sometimes I just really want you here,

I want you back.

But,

I know that's not our fate.

I honestly think you'll just be a memory.

I don't think we'll be in each other's lives.

Just another distant,
automatic,
numb,
"like"
on the social stream.

I thought you'd be that person,
I thought you were that person so quickly,

That maybe it was doomed from the beginning.

I fell into the spell.
Into your spell, right?

I know you thought you could try it.
I really hope you take the time for yourself.
I really hope you don't break another girl's heart.
I really hope I don't fall into another spell.

By you,
or anyone else.

I want to be mad at you.

I want to be mad at you for breaking my heart,
For pulling me along.

But, I understand.

And I can be mad if I want to.
I'm mad that I miss you right now.

I don't want to.

I'm mad that I want to hear your voice.
I'm mad that I want you here to just be.

To love.
To be in love.
To be the love and life
I thought we had.

But all of that was an illusion.

I know I wasn't.
I know deep down
you weren't.

But right now,
I don't want to believe that.

Right now,
I am aching,
I am hurting,
I am wanting my person back.

I want myself back.

I want a true love.

And I know someday,
I will have my person.

A person who is and isn't mine.
Who is life itself.
Who will grow and continue to grow.
Who loves and doesn't try to change me.

I want that for myself.
I want to do the same for myself.
I will love myself and give myself the love
that I deserve.

The love,
the love you couldn't provide.

The love,
that right now,
I still desperately ache for,

ache for from you.

I wonder how long I'll love you for.

I know it might change and shape over time.
But right now,
I know it's the kind of love that's not a "friend" love,
It's the kind of love where I wish you were here.
It's the kind of love where I think about your smile
and your goofy jokes.
It's the kind of love where I want to feel your arms
wrapped around me and hearing the beat of your
heart against your chest.
It's the kind of love where I want to hear your voice,
your laugh.
It's the kind of love where happy memories pop up
and it's like I'm right back there.
It's the kind of love that makes it hard to still accept
that you're not here anymore.
That I can't just call and say "I love you"
without having my heart torn in two.
I wonder why this love feels so hard to shape.
Shape into a more subtle,
"I wish you the best"
kind of love.

It's been three months now.
Three months since we said our goodbyes.
I reacted in ways I'm not proud of.
I apologize for my reactions,
but I don't apologize for my feelings.
The heartbroken pain I felt.
The pain I was trying to avoid by the reaction.
I apologize for that.
But if I didn't have that experience,
I wouldn't have noticed that pattern,
that reaction.
I wouldn't have reflected and learned and grown.
I wonder if you've been reflecting,
learning and growing.
I wonder if you're just as still in love as I am.
I hope that both of us can take this
as a loving corrective experience.
Part of me still hopes not.
A part of me still wants you to realize
the mistake you made and come find me.

But, I know deep down that if you did,
I don't think I'd accept it.
And deep down,
I don't think that would happen.
I still so very much love you.
Love the idea of having a partner to grow with.
I will have that someday.
Even if you are in my future or not.

Not matter how much time has passed

Or how much distance there is between us.

You will always have my best interest.

My love for you was true.

My pain of your loss is real.

I'm sorry for how I've been reacting.

I do not apologize for the feelings.

My heart is heavy.

Eventually, over time it will get better.

I hope by then we are both happy and in love
with life.

You always will have a space here with me.

What am I feeling?

I don't really understand.

Is this fear?
Grief?

It's definitely some sort of discomfort.

Is this growth?

Am I falling into and old pattern?

I don't understand really.

Maybe it's that part of me that wants to go back
to what hurt me.
And I don't want that.

Is that why I feel weird?
I fed that part of me that wants that comfort?

I don't want to keep doing that and I know
I will falter.
But I feel like maybe I faltered a little too much.

I don't owe my ex anything.

Do I want to maintain a relationship?
I do want to maintain some sort of civil agreement.
Which I think we did but I keep thinking my sister
will be disappointed in me.

Maybe because I'm disappointed with myself?

I don't want to fall into thinking something
can happen between us.
Because I know that will not happen
and that hope will keep me here.
Keep me from growing.
From becoming this beautiful,
amazing person.

Because I am fucking beautiful and amazing
and I'm also flawed
and stumble
and fall.

I'm imperfectly human
and I deserve another imperfect human
to provide me that space.
To be.

Maybe I do need to let this go.
I need to let him go.
I need to let go the idea of him go.

Because that will keep me from reaching my truth.

I think I don't want to continue contact.
And I can decide that and it can be that.

So bye lover.

Hope you finally choose to push through
your discomfort.
And I don't really want to be there to see it.
Sounds harsh but I got my life to focus on.

So bye.

I need growing people in my life.
Not those who are stuck.
So I'm leaving.
And I don't need to tell you.

I don't owe you anything but if you reach out,
Sure I'll say hi because I set that boundary.

Thanks for reaching out because it's showing me
that I don't really want to maintain you in my life.

Because I don't need that.

I'm starting to think I made a mistake...

I made a mistake coming here...
I made a mistake leaving...

I miss I guess feeling...
I miss being happy...
I miss my friends...
I miss feeling like a part of something...

Will that change?

Will I come to love this new space I'm in?

Or will I go back to you?

I'm still thinking about you.
How everything you wanted, is coming true for me.

Isn't it kind of funny how that works?

I wonder still how you're doing.
I try not to look you up because it pains me
still to see you.
But sometimes I think I need to.

To see if you have moved on.
If you're happy.
If you still think of me.

I'm in a really low place.
I don't think I've ever been this low before.
And I just miss everything I had.

I miss Denver.
I miss Colorado.
I miss the mountains.
I miss the sun.
I miss the people.
I miss you again.

I'm just aching to feel something other
than this depression.

How do I do that?
How do I move on?
I like to think that it's not just me.
Everything around us is collapsing.

I want to be happy here.
But all I want right now is what I use to know.
What I use to have.

What I thought,
would be mine.

What is keeping me?

Keeping me from allowing me to feel?
To fully feel?

It feels like I'm doing something without you.
That I'm betraying you.
That I had left you
and I'm not allowed to
build something new
without you.

It's like you'd be mad,
or sad,
or hurt.

That I did the worse thing possible.

But why does it matter?

When did you stop and think,
"I wish she was here,"
when you were climbing
with friends,
exploring the mountains,
meeting new people?

It's hard to believe you did.

Yet, I have this guilt.
This "I need to spend this,
memory,
time,
experience,
with you."

But, that's not us anymore.

Why am I so stuck in a "reality"
that's a fantasy?
Why is my vision blurred with false dreams?
Are they even dreams?

Why do I feel I need you?
That I need your permission to live?
That I need your permission to be?

That is not how love works.

I am not meant to fit your needs.

I am not meant to try and fit
into a puzzle that's not designed
for me.

And yet,
that's also what I did to you.

Unconsciously,
wanting,
needing,
craving,
you.

You to complete me.
You to soften the blow,
take my pain,
tell me "It's okay, I'll protect you."
When I needed to fight on my own.

But,
I was so scared to face it alone.
To face him alone.
To be alone in this consuming pain.

I'm sorry.
I'm sorry I dragged you down with it.
I'm sorry I didn't see it.
I'm sorry I thought I couldn't do it on my own.
It was not yours to take on.
It was never yours.
It was never mine.
And here we are both,
trying to break it.

Trying to heal a wound that's as old as time.
A wound that was projected.
Forced into our reality.
Twisting our conception of truth.
Twisting our conception of love.

I'm sorry we both have a broken pattern.
I'm sorry we both have to build ourselves out.
I'm sorry.
I'm sorry.
I'm sorry.

But most of all,
I am sorry for myself.

For not trusting in my ability.
In my power.
For not recognizing my fiery strength.

And that I am not alone.

That I am whole.

That I have been pushed so far away from myself,
I lost the path back.

And I'm starting to think I found it.

I found the rocks and pebbles,
the trails and sunlight,
coming back to you.
To me.
To Arlyne.

You

are a home I've always known,
and a place I've never been to.

(love)

My inner child is speaking.

She feels abandoned by you.
She feels abandoned by the world.

Why didn't you love me?
Why didn't anyone help me?
Why didn't anyone see the tears?
The fear?

Why didn't anyone stop and say,
"Are you okay?"

Why didn't anyone care?
Why didn't anyone notice?
Why didn't anyone tell me,
"You'll be okay",
"you are loved",
"I won't hurt you."

Why didn't you stay?
Why did you leave me?
Why did you leave me,
in all this pain?
Why couldn't you see me?
Why couldn't you love me?

Why couldn't you be there for me?

Was I not enough?
Was there something wrong with me?
Was I the problem?
Am I the problem?

That's why they leave right?
That's why they hurt me.
That's why they left me alone.
That's why you couldn't stay.

You left me.
You denied me.
You punished me.
For being true.
For being me.

Because I'm the problem.

How do I teach my inner child love without guidance?
Without a model?

Do I even know what love is?

When I touch it,
will it burn me?
Or will it be the same?
The same as it was before?
Or will it be freeing?
Free to take charge,
free to be,
free for me to be me.

I know why we attracted each other.

We completed a pattern.

Mine, seeking safety.
Yours, seeking completion.

A combination for disaster.
A combination for dependency.
A combination no longer needed.
No longer needed in our timelines.

You showed me what it meant to connect.
To connect fully and deeply with yourself.
To find the joy,
the love,
the light of this life.

With a connection that starts with you.
Your inner you.

You showed me what it was like to find love.
A truer love than I had experienced.

One that didn't have me question my sanity.
One that validated and built trust.
One that may have been different if we were
different.

At different timelines and spaces.
Different moments of our lives.
Different stars among the universes.

But we weren't.

That's not us.

We were to collide and point in different directions.
Swerve into our legacy.
Fall into uncertainty.
Uncertainty of ourselves,
of our futures,
of what was to become of us...

nothing.

We were meant to be nothing.

Nothing of us,
nothing of them,
nothing of we,

Nothing.

I feel like I'm the toxic one.

I've always been.

I'm the one that needs fixing.
I'm the one that needs saving.
Because I can't do it on my own.
And that makes me the toxic one.

Do you ever get in a panic,
when I post about friends
and you think I've moved on?

Do you delete your Instagram
just to get some space?
To calm down your nerves
and tell yourself your safe?

Do you ever think about me
as you're crying on your bedroom floor?

Do you ever think of me?

Do you ever think about how I'm just fine
and that sends you into a spiral?

That maybe if you were better
or good enough,
that you'd be here to stay?

Or if you had tried harder,
You would have made it work?

But then I think,
No,
those thoughts never happen for you.
You are in a much better space.

And because I'm here writing to you,
that I'm the toxic one.
I've always been.

I want to burn

your name off
my chest
and replace
it with
love notes
from you

so that I will
no longer
have to carry
the burden of
speaking your
name.

(tattoos)

At first,

I thought I made a mistake reaching back out.

About 2 weeks later,
I had a flood of emotions come bubbling up
and I didn't know what to do with it.

I wanted to push it back down,
run away,
and escape.

I knew that I did not want to do that this time around.
I knew that if I did,
I would never work through this.

These displaced emotions and feelings that were not
meant to be placed on you
or our relationship.

I've been working really hard to work through them.
To remind myself of the truth and not what the
betrayal,
abandonment,
and shame
were trying to have me believe.

As much as I know that our time together was short,
I still feel and believe it was something special.

We may have both been hurting,
which I feel may initially brought us together,
and there was more to that.

There was connection,
and vulnerability,
and love.

There was the want to understand.
Fully and deeply.

You were a lot of firsts for me,
Especially coming from a traumatic past.

I appreciate you still allowing space for me,
even as I had so desperately tried to push you away.
What we had experienced away.
Because it was so painful having to lose something,
someone,
I was not ready to lose.

I thought it would be easier to pretend
it never happened.
That it was never meant to happen.

I am grateful I tried again.

I reached out and had these emotions come in.

This time I could name them and provide them space.
This time I feel I can allow you space.
The space you so generously provided me.

Thank you,
again,
Thank you for seeing me.

Thank you for teaching me space and forgiveness.

Thank you.

I have a strong urge to reach out to you.

Let you know I'm thinking about you.

But I'll write instead.

I want to let you know you still cross my mind,
almost every day.

I thought of getting you a gift.

I thought of getting you a gift like old times.

Sometimes I wonder if you ever think that same thing.
You see something in a store window and think,
"she would like this"
and a smile will sneak across your face.

I wonder if you're thinking of that now,
as you're with family or friends,
or even a new love.

I wonder if you are happy and having a good time.
If you're loving life and feel like you found your path.

I guess this is me still saying I love you,
and think of you,
and want so much for you.

You were such a light in a dark time for me.

I want to tell you how much I appreciate you.
How much I still do,
how much I still want to and if you do too.

I guess what I want to say is,
Thank you,
I love you,
I appreciate you,
and Merry Christmas.

I don't know what else I would write

besides that,
I want you,
right now
and forever.

Happy New Year.

It's weird to think that this time last year,
we were drinking champagne,
dancing the night away,
and deeply in love,
not caring about tomorrow,
not aware of the months ahead.

That this time this year,
we'd be thousands of miles away from each other.
Without one phone call.
Without one text.
Without one
"I love you"
or
"I miss you."

I'm sure you've made plans to do
something fun with friends.
A small get together to celebrate life,
freedom,
and joy.

I like to think that you're making plans
with someone else.
Someone new,
to dance the night away
and forget about life for a while.

I think it's easier to imagine you with someone new
because maybe if you're over me,
maybe I can finally be over you.

I still get anxiety of potentially stumbling
upon an image of you,
happy and in love with someone else.

As much as I want that for you,
I fear it may also break me.

But,
I am also deserving of that new life too.

I just need to release you.

Why are you so hard to let go?
Why do I still cling on in hopes that you feel
the same way as I do?
Hoping,
wondering,
wanting.
Wanting to be back with me.
And wanting to be back with you.

Almost a year later,
and I know that's not our fate.

You will be with friends
and maybe a new love.

I will be here with family.

And we won't speak,
or call,
or text.

We'll just pretend that our hearts aren't torn
and we're not missing each other.

Well,
that is what I hope.

But you can feel differently.

You can be over me.
You can be happy and in love
with someone else.

And I'll be here,
working on moving past,
working on loving me again.

Loving me and being with me
because I deserve it.

I deserve to be loved too.
To be cherished.
To have the space to be me.

But right now,
I'm crying and hurting for you.

I am wanting so badly to feel your touch,
To hear your words of love.

Right now,
I just want you,
I want what I thought was us
and stay in that moment
until I wake up.

I was so in love with you,

so infatuated by you.

Everything about you.

Every freckle on your skin,
every wrinkle on your face,

completely and hopelessly
enamored in you.

(consumed)

You weren't perfect,

but you damn sure tired.

(practice makes perfect)

I will forever be grateful

for the small time
the universe graced us.

To have found
one another amongst the chaos
and share
together in our
little infinity.

(infinite)

You were my first taste

of all the things
I've ever wanted.

And that is why
it has been so hard
to let you go.

(stuck)

Every time I write to you

it feels like there's
never enough words
or phrases
to portray what
I really want to say to you.

All the words have been
used up,
all the phrases repeated,
yet, I feel like I'm
not done yet.
Telling you my thoughts,
writing out my stories.

I feel pressured to find
the perfect thing to say,
to sum up everything
that's been shared.

And maybe there won't be.

Maybe there won't be a perfect ending,
a perfect way to say goodbye.

A time where I will be satisfied
with the ending.

Maybe I won't feel satisfied
with my final letter to you.

Maybe I won't be done writing to you
And maybe that's fine.

Maybe that's what I need
to somehow keep a piece of you with me.

I wonder if you still think about our song.

Do you still think about
that night?

When we danced and sang
in the shower,
your forehead against mine
as you sang
"Beautiful Stranger,"
against my lips?

Do you remember how much
I cried when I told you
I loved you?

How afraid I was
to drown you with me
in the chaos of my mind?

When I told you
how I thought you
were mine,
as we lay
under the covers
of my bed?

How I still trust and
believe you still feel
the same?

I wonder if when you hear
our song,
if it takes you back
to the love we lost
buried underneath
uncertainty and shame.

The love that I still
foolishly fuel,
keeping the light on,
waiting,
in hopes
of your return.

I realize now,

that all these
letters to you
are my final
goodbyes,
my final "I love yous"
and "you are mine."

My final attempts
to understand
what happened
and what's next.

My final connections
to a love
I thought
would be mine,
what I thought
would be ours
to share amongst
the universes
with our chests
puffed high as

we howled into
the night
the love song of life.

The letters are my way
of coping,
accepting that you
are no longer mine,
you were never mine
and you will always
be lover.

You will always be
a little moment
frozen in time
among these pages
forever sharing the
love that we hold,
that we held for one another.

That even in love,
there are endings,
endings with difficult
decisions and shared tears,

endings that didn't seem
fair or logical at the time
but are now the beginnings
of something so much more.

That love does not disappear.
It shifts.
It morphs into something
small
like a bud of a flower,
waiting for the water
the sunshine of connection
to bloom into a new love,

a new lover.

Have you ever

stopped to think
that maybe
we both
needed each other?

That we were meant
to gravitate toward one another
for a reason?

That the stars aligned,
and sparks flew
and we collided
in a chemical imbalance
called love?

We needed each other,
to stumble
and fall,
to learn
and unlearn
to witness the beauty
and the pain to be human.

To watch the one we
love suffer
just to see them
blossom.

We were meant to be
the distraction,
the distraction we needed
to look within,
to see our flaws
and imperfections
the trauma still felt
and the love that we'd
lost.

We were meant to
catch fire,
ignite into a burning
flame,
that eventually
gave out.

We were meant to feel
the toxins
the chemicals
envelope our brains,
feel the sparks
and the trembles
beneath our skin.

We were meant to
be there,
to share in the space
that was ours.

We were meant to
come together just
so we could fall apart
just so we could
come back together,
pick up our pieces
and change our perspective.

You were meant to break my heart.
You were meant to break my cycle.
You were meant to hold my hand

and tell me you'd never leave me.
You were meant to go.
You were meant to let me grow.

You were meant to show me I can do it.

I can break the cycle.
I can find a healthier love.
I can finally be me.

That I don't need to
hide anymore,
behind the trauma
and the fear.

That I can be loved
fully and deeply,
that someone will
try and understand me.

That I can be seen.

Because that's all I've ever wanted.

That's all I've ever wanted
and you
granted me that
and I know
I can do it again.

I know I can try again.
This time,
a little wiser
and a little more healed.

And I hope the same for you.

Because otherwise,

what was our love for?

You're coming to mind

a lot recently
and I'm not sure
why

sometimes I think
I get it

a year ago we had
just broken up

sometimes,

I go back
to that day
like it was yesterday

there was an aching
in my chest where
my heart use to be

she couldn't understand
what was happening
why you chose to leave
me.

There were moments
when I didn't know
how to breathe

suffocating in the
loss of a broken
heart

it's weird to think
that maybe
if I just
write about it

that you'll feel it too

suddenly,

the world gets heavy
and you think of me
you wonder how I'm
doing and if I'm
safe

you'll think about all

the times that we laughed
and couldn't stop from
loving each other

but

I know that won't
happen

you won't feel my
pain

my hurt

you'll go on about
your day
without
a care in the world
and I'll be here
reliving the pain
when you walked
away

and I know

I make it dramatic

(I am a poet)

because I know it
was not that simple
for you

your fears got the
best of you
and over fed it

your discomfort to
change got the better
of you and I
get it

I get it

because that was

me

For so long

before you.

I was afraid to try

again

I was afraid of
being hurt

I was afraid of

letting someone in
and I did

I let you in

I let you in to
see the dark parts
of my past
and all I can feel
is that you left it

you left it

because

I reminded you
that pain needs
to be felt
to move past it
and that's scary
it's terrifying

so I get it

I understand

yet it doesn't

explain why

I hold on to the

doubt that

you never truly

cared

and I was used

in your journey

to self-empowerment.

Why?

What happened?

What happened the day you saw him?
The day you came with me to the hearing?
It's like something in you switched
and I could never understand why.

Did he remind you of someone?

Did he remind you of yourself?

Did you think I was weak to be afraid of someone?

That you couldn't be with someone
who couldn't stand up for herself?

If so,
you're wrong.

I did stand up for myself.

I said no to him,
I said no to the abuse
I said no to you.

Maybe...

Tell me what happened,
tell me you felt it, you shifted.

You shifted away from me,
like I was the problem.

That was the day I felt the most shift in distance
from you.

Suddenly,
I was suffocating you.

When I feel,
all I did
was try to protect you
and have you understand
by communicating
my anxiety
my trauma
and understanding
that you and it were separate
that I and it were separate.

Yet, you didn't trust me
you didn't trust that I wouldn't do the same to you

turn on you
make you the bad guy.

And honestly,

I sort of did.

I was so mad at you for breaking my heart
I wanted you out of my life.

I wanted you so far away from me
and to leave me alone.

I wanted you to feel what I felt.

I wanted you to feel the heart break

I wanted you to be suffering with me

but you weren't

or you were

and I don't know

And I don't know if I ever will.

We were just two broken people

trying to find love
in the brokenness
of another.

(incomplete)

I threw away the letters

you gave me...

I wanted you to know that

the one you gave me
the day I was sick
and you told me you loved me
and
the one on
valentine's day
where I felt your
words were
more forced
less feeling
just needed to do it
because it was the
"right thing"

I threw them away
because
I knew keeping
them
reading the words
the thoughts

you had for me
would continue
to ignite the flame
that you'd come back
to me
and that flame
filled my lungs with
smoke
and created
more destruction
than easing
the pain
or understanding
that a person can
fully and deeply
love you one day
and ignore you
the next.

You were the song I needed

to get through
the darker chapters
of my life

(muse)

I feel like if I give you up

I'm giving up on myself.

Like everything I've worked for
will be nothing
because you're not there
to share it with.

It's like if I give up on you
then who am I?

Who am I to say
that we can't be?

Who am I to say
that we are better off
together?

Who am I to say
you are the one
who needs to stay?

I am still oh so attached to you.

Attached to the idea
of who you are
of what I want
of what was to become
of us.

And I fear that if I let you go
then I let our love go.

That I never truly loved you
and that we weren't true.

It feels like I'm trying to push past you
leave you behind.
Forget that you existed.

How do I honor our time together
without wanting you too?

That's where I'm stuck right now
of allowing you the space to be
to find new love
and grow.

Because that's what love is.

It is free of attachment
and full of space.

Space to be,
to be seen,
to grow
and evolve.

So why am I so stuck
on the idea
that if I let you go
our love wasn't real?

You became the inner voice I craved,

when the voice I needed
was within me this whole time

(how I say goodbye)

You used me

in hopes
of finding yourself

(crutch)

I am punishing myself

Why?

I am still chasing on to the hope
that if I fix myself

you will take me back

just like before

when we were together

when I was at my weakest
I tried my hardest
to make myself better

so that you wouldn't
have to suffer

so that you would
accept me

because you couldn't stand
to see me weak

because weakness is meek
and silence is honored

but that's your story
not mine

and yet I took that on

wrote it down with my blood

took it down into my soul

and said,
"this is mine now"

and I still carry it

I still carry your story

like I carried my mother's

like I carried his

like I carried on with everyone before

because then
I was liked

I was safe

I was acceptable

I was finally
a piece of the puzzle

I was labeled
and shipped off

but that wasn't me

and this isn't me

your story is not mine

so why did you give it to me?

Why did you place it on me?

I don't want it

This is not mine to hold

it is yours

it is yours to work through

not me

get this poison
        out
        of
        me

This does not belong
        to
        me

It is not mine to carry on.

It is yours, lover

It has always been

yours.

I had a dream you were with me

well, not really
but you were there

we were at a party
of some sort

and you were with your
partner

and I was with mine

and we were older,

I was maybe 30 or 29

and you came across the
room to me

in a blue suit with golden
leaves

and I waved hello
like everything between us
was fine

and you asked for my hand
to help you with your
cufflinks

and I did it without
hesitation

and we talked like we
were best friends

and I admitted I still wanted you

and you drew me close

and didn't let go

and I knew then that

I may always love you
and I need to release you

and that you may be
the first person
I need to remove myself from

not because I don't care

but because

I care

too deeply.

One day,

you'll think of me

how my hair
twirls and
glows in the
sunlight,

how I always
smile with
my whole face.

How I can
never seem
to stop singing

how I would
bury my face
in your chest
and tell you
I loved you

how I was
a mixture
of rain and
sunshine

and so
many secrets
and worries
that needed
a gentle
touch to
bring me
back to
shore,

how I gave you
all of my love
and you,

you gave me
all of yours.

(when you think of me)

I think we were supposed to be friends...

I think we were supposed to fall in love
long after our friendship began

because that's what I miss the most

I miss telling you about my day
and always wanting to know yours

I miss contemplating the philosophies of life
and becoming lost in your words

I miss playful banter and belly laughter
in your room,
in your apartment

I miss you

or what I thought was you

because when I really think about it,

those were the moments

I felt closest to you...

There are moments

when I'm happy
or sad
that you come to mind
and I wish
you were there
to share in that moment
so I can tell you my secrets
and you can tell me yours
and we'd be forever in the moment
and all will be yours

(wish you were here)

I have every right to be mad at you,

I have every right to be angry
hurt,
sad

I have every right to take my time getting over you

Because although it may not have meant
that much to you

it meant the world to me.

(I can take my time)

May we both

forgive each other

for the broken
hearts

ripped up
notes

and words
left unspoken.

(I'm sorry)

Someday,

you will be just a distant
memory

of a time

I didn't trust in my
own ability.

(someday)

I miss you a lot right now

I keep thinking about
New Year's night

when you were drunk and
so in love

how you would laugh at
the tiniest of things

and you just couldn't keep
your eyes off me.

You held me close
      snuggled your nose
      against mine
      and kissed me softly
      on the cheek
      whispering
      how much you
      loved me

and I felt it,

I felt it lover.

I felt it like I know
my own name

it was so deep
and pure
and like magic

I couldn't understand just
how lucky I was
to be loved by you

and to truly feel it

to not have someone
intoxicated
high
and telling me how
terrible I am
how I am the problem,
everything is my fault

you granted me such
a different love
and I don't know if
either of us were ready
for it.

And all I know
is that
right now

I want that love

I want to feel it again

to my core

that someone sees me

someone loves me

and I wanted that to
be you

and I know now

that might have to wait

and it might never be

from you

again.

Is there a reason I can't let you go?

I still feel childish
that I'm holding on
and sometimes I feel
like I don't know why
that I'm just making up
how much I want you
and that's not true

I start to spiral into
shaming myself
and I think that's
what's continuing the cycle

and that's what's keeping
me from processing
and letting go
and just being okay
with you not being here
that you're no longer
mine even though you
were never mine
and
I think it's because
I feel that if I let

this go,
I fear I won't find
another like this again

that I will fall back
to a toxic love
and that I will never
break the cycle
and if I break it
with you
then everything will
work out

but it's me who
needs to break it
within myself

it has always been me.

I think the hardest

thing to accept
is that
you never
loved me,

you just thought you did.

(false dreams)

Things I want to say to you...

I want to tell you that
I've been reflecting a lot

Reflecting on how,
why,
what went wrong

and I realized there
were a couple
things that remain
true,

I fell completely
head over heels
for you

and

it hurt like hell
to let you go

now,

over a year later
and as my mind goes
back to a time I
felt the happiest,
it was always a matter
of time before
we lost it.

We rushed it,

we got so excited to
have found a person
who embodied what we
were looking for,
we quickly grabbed on
and held on tight

not realizing
our relationship crumbled
before it even began

and even so
there was so much to
release of you
in the short span
we had.

And if one thing
is for certain
the trust I
had built for you
still stands true,

even now as I write this,
I still trust
that you will be on
my team,

rooting for me
on the side lines,

always willing to have
a chat and catch up

and for some time
I was taken aback
at the amount of
trust I had for
you

which was also
difficult in letting you
free.

But,

I think the most
important thing
you had taught me
was that no matter
who I was
or how broken
I was
that there are
people
who are willing
to understand

a gift I will forever
be grateful for.

Thank you.

Thank you for trying
to understand me
when I was
still trying
to understand
myself.

You are a part of

me that I need
to accept

because not loving
you
means not loving
me.

(acceptance)

I think I am finally releasing you.

And a part of me thinks it's funny
that a 3-month relationship
took over a year to get over.

But here's why...

You were not the only thing,
you were not the only person
I was trying to release.

You see...

you became my anchor

my ball and chain
that kept me from floating
into space

kept me from completely
losing sight of who I am

because (I don't know if you noticed but)
I was on full survival mode.

I was just surviving

I was going through the motions
of what it meant to be
human

and you

you reminded me that life is precious
and people are complicated
and hurt and pain can look different for each person

I was drawn to you
for a number of reasons
but I think the most
important one is
how you reminded me
of what it meant
to be

I was drawn to you because
you reminded me of who
I could be

of who I am
beyond the need for survival.

You reminded me
of what it means
to let people in
to trust in yourself,
in your healing

and that you do not need
to be fully healed
to be fully loved

you reminded me
of all those things
and when you were gone
so was my worth

I unconsciously
placed my worth
of who I am
who I could be
and my love
on to you

and it makes sense
it makes sense why
it took so long to move forward
to release you

because you were the push
I needed to recognize
I was breathing in water
when the rest of us
were breathing air.

I forgive you.

I forgive you
for unsuccessfully
trying to fall
in love again

with me.

(I set you free)

author's note

Here she is! Book number two! I can't believe we are here! This is the second poetry collection of the three-book series, and it was such a whirlwind reading through this work again and sharing with you all. This collection holds my letters to someone I truly loved. This person came into my life shortly after the end of my traumatic relationship and it was profound. I fell so deeply in love with this person. They were the first person I felt truly loved and adored by and losing them was absolutely devastating. I spiraled and tried everything in my power to block the waves of love from flowing through me. But, as hard as I tried, the stones that I piled up from the heartbreak, grief, anger, hurt, and shame could not stop the flow of love from seeping through. The love found the cracks and crevasses of self-compassion, forgiveness and acceptance and made her way out. I learned through that breakup that you cannot block the raging waters of love. Because no matter what, the water will always flow to love.

Thank you so much for continuing to follow me on my journey and picking up this book! I am so excited for you all to witness the final work of my journey home.

I hope you enjoyed my little words.

acknowledgements

I want to provide a special shout out to some incredible people who made this second book possible.

To David, I have no idea if you will ever read this but thank you for showing me what it truly means to love. I will forever be grateful to you for our little time together.

To my interior and cover design editor Rein, you have such an amazing ability to put my ideas into a beautiful creation that truly feels like me. Thank you for now a second beautiful book.

To my roommate and dear friend Vanessa, thank you for all your support on my first collection. You are like the second "mother" I've never had, and I am so grateful to you and your love for me and my creative endeavors. Thank you for showing me what it means to be a mama.

Lastly, thank you to everyone else behind the scenes, who hasn't been named, in being a part of making this book possible. To my therapists, friends, and family. Thank you. This book would not have been possible without your support. I appreciate you all.

about the author

Arlyne is a self-published storyteller, spirit dancer, womb carrier, and Chicana from Denver, Colorado. Arlyne has been writing since she was a little womb and has found poetry to be a powerful way to creatively express herself and share her story with the world. Along with this book, Arlyne is the author of *letters i'll never send*, her debut poetry collection. She hopes that sharing her words will bring a sense of belonging and touch the hearts of others. Arlyne lives an artful and happy life in her lovely Denver home with her dear friend Vanessa, Vanessa's son Oliver, and their pets, Koko, Ruby, Jude and some fish.

@tecuani_cihuatl
@tecuani_cihuatl

www.ingramcontent.com/pod-product-compliance
Lightning Source LLC
Chambersburg PA
CBHW052012150726
47999CB00004B/1627